The Propriety of Weeding

Colin Will

RED SQUIRREL

First published in the UK in 2012 by
Red Squirrel Press
Briery Hill Cottage
Stannington
Morpeth
Northumberland
United Kingdom
NE61 6ES
www.redsquirrelpress.com

Red Squirrel Press is distributed by Central Books and
represented by Inpress Ltd.
www.inpressbooks.co.uk

A CIP catalogue record is available from The British Library.

ISBN: 978-1-906700-61-4

Printed by Martins the Printers
Sea View Works
Spittal
Berwick-upon-Tweed
United Kingdom
TD15 1RS

Acknowledgments

Versions of some of these poems have been published in
Ambit, Drey, Z$_2$O, Northwords Now, Iota, Gutter, Eildon
Tree, Poetry Scotland, Snakeskin, qarrtsiluni, Strawberries:
poems in honour of Edwin Morgan, a handful of stones,
World Haiku Review, Broadside, St Abbs Community
website, Bolts of Silk, By Grand Central Station We Sat
Down and Wept (ed. K Cadwallender), Split Screen (ed.
A. Jackson), Inspired? Get Writing (National Galleries of
Scotland), Working Words (ed. J.S. Savage). Field Notes was
commissioned by Alastair Cook for a filmpoem with the
same title.

As always, thanks to Jane for her support.

The dull necessity of weeding arises, because every healthy plant is a racist and an imperialist; every daisy (even) wishes to establish for itself an Empire on which the sun never sets.

Ian Hamilton Finlay

Contents

Making a Garden

As you know, a true Garden has four elements.
Rocks soar at the back; piles of lake-worn limestone,
eroded into pocks and hollows, stacked up high
as in the Emperor's Hill of Accumulated Elegance.
There are those in Chengde who manufacture rocks
of surpassing beauty, if you cannot afford
the natural ones from Tai Hu.

Water is essential, for reflection when still,
for music when moving; to accept
the wind's fingertips and to broadcast ripples.
Fish are optional. Turtles may help focus
on longevity, but they too may be omitted.
It is a delight to observe the bubbling of new water
through stones, and humbling to contemplate
the profundity of wells.

Buildings belong in Gardens,
for they are places of people, for people.
They shade the hot sun in summer
and the dismal rains of autumn.
Here you may sit, take tea, admire
your achievement, paint, compose poems,
play sweet music, drink with friends.

Plants fill the spaces between rocks and water,
carpeting, screening, creating vistas of nature.
Some must be tall to take the eye to the region of birds.
Others are low, to edge a stone path, drift over walls.
Dragon walls should never be covered.
In the appropriate season grow flowers, but be sparing
with your palette, for the colour of plants is green.

Be thoughtful, be patient, spend outrageously.

In the Gardens of China

The Garden of Assembled Perfumes
The Master of the Nets' Garden
The Garden of Exuberant Spring
Sufficiency Garden
The Garden of Harmonious Interest
The Garden of Moonlit Fertility
The Humble Administrator's Garden
Folded Brocade Hill
Incense Burner Peak
Longevity Hill
The Hill of Accumulated Elegance
Vast Bright Lake
The Fish-knowing Bridge
Large Western Heaven
Islands of the Immortals
The Temple of Happy Meditation
The Temple of the Azure Clouds
The Altar of the Land and Grain
The Hall of Prayer for Good Harvests
The Travelling Palace of Upholding Heaven
The Well of the Pearl Concubine
The Terrace for Receiving Dew
The Pavilion of Admirable Fragrance
The Pavilion of Literary Depth
The Pavilion of the Reposing Clouds
The Studio of Introspection
Water Cloud Kiosk
The Lodge of the Propriety of Weeding

Seed

Destiny is already here in a thread of forces;
plans to make cell or tree, poison or cure.

We read the sequence of knots
in each spliced strand,
or try to fathom the album of the world
from desiccated pages,
but forest walks still surprise with joy;
and how many lives have started
among the scent of blossoms?

More than cataloguers know,
for growers create more
than a list of passions.

Fresno stopover

Late-night swim in hotel pool,
lights round shallow-end tables;
Spanish voices liquidise the day's events
in quiet, evening laughter,
as we make hushed splashes
in the cooling water.

Woken up, breakfasted, bags loaded,
back on the bus,
we pass blocks of almond trees, pecans,
to a farm stall, stocking up for lunch
on the fruits of Fresno fields,
harvested yesterday. Crops of pickers
move steadily North
as the seasons drift
to the apples of Washington.

The new one
(Neon)

From chilled liquid air
three gases boiled off –
the strange one, the hidden one,
and the new one.

Injected into pumped-out glass tubes
it glows orange-red, and very brightly,
when a current's passed. Did anyone count
the numbers of new cars sold
thanks to words made of light?

If nobility comes from disdaining attachments,
then call it noble, but it's a sterile aristocracy
with no family, no descendants,
all shells filled, and no spare hands
to hold.

El Dorado

Suilven's struck by the last shaft of sunset
and turns to gold. I've seen it before,
but that doesn't diminish the awe
we all feel, dashing out over the wet grass
with cameras, braving the clouds
of inevitable midges, to make this moment
permanent.

At the far end of the loch
lines of perspective narrow to a focus
where we watch a golden hind cross
the mountain's gold reflection,
casting sheets of water into the air
as if in slow motion.

Suilven's basement too is made of gold,
and across the glen the ancient pyramid
of Canisp has the same lustrous hue.

Then we turn to each other and find
we too are transformed by this light;
hair and faces transmuted
into sheets and filaments of the element
Midas would have known, and each of us
with a halo – biting flecks of gold.

Father of Sky
(Uranium)

Son-husband of Gaia,
father of the Titans,
this mythic metal
flaunts his instability
with a half-life as long
as the age of the Sun.

Seven kilos to destroy a city,
shaped charges at the heart
of Little Boy blew the blocks together,
ignited the fireball that melted
the people of Hiroshima –
some Sky; some Father.

Forty years later we sat
in our Comrie caravan
watching Band Aid
under the heavy rain
we didn't know was dripping debris
from Chernobyl, poisoning
the lichens with caesium 137.

What was left – melted core –
still slowly creeps down through the crust
under its leaky sarcophagus,
a lithospheric time-bomb.

How beautiful, the colours
of uranium glass, ceramic glazes,
but no-one drinks now
from these ticking chalices.
Atomic clocks fission time
into heartbeats of slow neutrons.

Identity theft

The sanderlings are tiny fairies, dancing, wave dodging;
last week it was elephant doves crowding the sparrows
off the bird table. Tomorrow she'll trawl again
through the wreckage of language, make links
from random connections. The structure holds,
the same certainty of syntax prevails,
but there's a whimsy in her choice of nouns
and what-you-call-its – describing words.
She's going down, for the third long time,
into that slow acid bath, the fizzing soup
which splits word from world, knowledge from memory.
It's a soft dissolve, like sculpture running backwards
until the armature emerges, then that too
corrodes, breaks down, and floats away.

Just touch

Is it day? Is it night? What's the difference.
I hold my hand out, but the air feels
neither warm nor cold. What's the difference?
I stumble across the space. This time I don't
hit anything. Yesterday, if it was yesterday,
if today had a before or if it meant
anything, I felt a sharp pain in
my knee, as if I'd struck something,
a hard something, a something with edges.
I thought today, if today has any meaning,
if the present means anything, it might
strike me again, and I'd know I was
in the same place again, as if 'again' means
anything, as if anything in this place,
whatever place means, means anything. Stumble.
That's the word, if the word explains, describes
or otherwise justifies the reality of movement,
if movement has any significance, as if the
journey across this space from birth to
death, has anything worthwhile to say.
Stumble. Pain. No pain. Whatever pain
is. Stumble. Nothing. Today.

Finding family

Our plots take up
so little space,
our headstones' footprints
even less, save the prone ones,
whose words are picked out
in moss, or worn smooth
by careless feet and
care-even-less weather.

I'm suddenly aware
I'm standing on what's left
of two ancestors, and the shock
of seeing my wife's name here -
shared with a great great
whatever grandmother -
takes my breath away.

This is Longside, near Lonmay,
not far from Crimond and Rora,
north of Ellon, south-east of Pitsligo,
Strichen and New Deer,
a few miles from Foveran
and the other places I never knew,
places where their names were known,
their heart-shaped heartland.

It's a land dotted with cairns
and stone circles, Pictish carvings,
huge skies, short sturdy beasts
in the neat fields and folk
well at themselves, standing up
against the constant wind.

The useful, everyday lives
of farmhands, roadmen
skivvies and souters,
as vital then as today's oilmen
receiving messages beamed
from Mormond Brae.

Missing

David Will was the first name I read,
same name as my first son.
I breathed again after a long gasp.
Missing, and the date and place.
Regiment: Gordon Highlanders of course,
because that's the one they all joined,
the ones from Buchan, the hinterland
behind the coastal towns, places
my forebears lived and laboured.

Remains not found or identified,
fragments of anonymous bone,
strips of nameless flesh,
meat for the trench rats, a red stain
in the puddles that quickly dribbled
into pools of mud, churned by incoming shells
or the boots of marching men.

John Will was next, and in the lists
another John, four Jameses,
a Duncan (my other son's name),
two brothers, William and George.
Grandmother's maiden name produced
a new batch, adding Mutch to Will,
folk from Strichen and the Newburgh.

Twenty-five names in all, men who travelled
from Huntly to Ypres, Ellon to Cambrai,
and did not come home. My grandfather made shoes
in Aberdeen and Edinburgh, never spoke
about his service, but he marched back
and fathered my father, the year after
hostilities ended, but didn't.

Walled gardens feature frequently
in this landscape, each with their strange crops:
ranks of identical upright slabs
with simple inscriptions, books of lists.
Planting poppied crosses doesn't work for me;
commemorating isn't what I want to do.
I try to make personal connections, but I can't.

That happened later in a farmer's field.
A drainage ditch in the chalky soil
had opened an unmapped trench,
and in the bottom we found bullets,
a belt buckle, and a few white bones:
a shiny rib, and the smooth head of a femur.

Watching birds

"10,124 Pinkfoot Geese sighted at Aberlady,"
read the note on the whiteboard.
10,124 eh? A big number; a lot
of counting, and so precise.

I picture the counter's thumb,
swollen and tired from an excess
of clicking, eyes blearing across
the grey-brown flock. "Did I count
that group? Has that goose moved?"

I can't imagine devotion
on this scale. It's enough
that I recall walking
in a November dusk
through the buckthorn thicket,
foot before unseen foot
along the muddy path.

Over my head
10,124 Pinkfoot Geese babbled
in the near darkness.
This glorious chorus came and went
in waves, as V after V
whiffled in to land
on the salt flats.

I don't read anything
into this; it's a fact, an event
that occurs every evening,
witnessed or not.
I'm just glad to know
these visitors pause here,
their holiday home
in the warm Scottish winter.

Cabbage Water

Overhead, the same wind I can't hear
pushes the grey cottony masses
of cloud south, towards the wedge
of the Lammermuirs. All the weight
of vertical miles of atmosphere
presses down, constrains the air mass
so the particles of pinpoint water
pressure-squeeze closer, start
to coalesce around a shower curtain
of rain, a chain reaction, growing heavy,
falling faster, like window drops
becoming window streams.

Dry earth spits dust, puffballs release spores,
tiny brown smokes. I remember hearing
the first welcome rattle on cabbages,
how the waxy leaves grew globes
of magnifying water, each with a sunflash
just above the lower margin. We looked
for the sunsource, found it in a glare-patch
of brighter sky.

The hook

It was the room under the roof
so in summer we sweltered.
Lying in bed, knowing we wouldn't sleep
until we no longer worried about not sleeping.
The sweat oozed between our bodies
and the sheet below. Sex, of course,
was out of the question, all contact shunned.

The moon rose in the corner
of the Velux window, a white
pie segment, growing into
a silver pizza. I remembered,
as if I'd only just forgotten,
that there was a latch
on the window frame, that somewhere
was a pole with hook on the end,
a hook that only fitted that latch
and nothing else.

I rose from my side of the bed,
causing a new spring of moisture
from my back, the backs of my thighs.
The glory hole, the scullery cupboard,
was where we stashed the things
we thought we'd never need,
and there it was. I stood
on the bed, unlatched the window
and let in the moon-conditioned air.

In the map gaps

By the time I reach the mobile
the caller's hung up. I stare
at the missed call number,
willing it to form a pattern
I might recognise. I don't
return the call, in case it's someone
from one of those mythical kingdoms –
West Anglia, North Saxonland,
the South Riding of Yorkshire.
Some nights the wind comes
from a direction that doesn't exist,
and there are voices in it
that I know are crying.

The love song of the Sensory Homunculus

Ignore the surface appearance –
you coped with Quasimodo after all –
concentrate on essentials.

My lips can trace a symphony
on your skin, reflecting its warmth,
its satin high notes, sandalwood curves.

My tongue tastes salt sweat,
savours sweetness and
the hot licks of umami.

My nose detects each dab
of fragrance, behind the ears, and
those foxy puffs that make it quiver.

I hear your marimba ribs expand,
a little lower lung crepitation,
your breathy words excite me.

My best features? Hands, natch,
not monstrous, made to multiply
the range and forms of touch.

Allow me, if you will, to use them
to palm your body, admire your textures,
fingertip your slippy tresses, typologies

of skin, dry or moist, smooth or squamous,
little catches of stubble, lushnesses of groin,
flushes of neck and chest, all the swells and dips

of one who matches my cortical map
in most respects, else analogues
our most intimate connectors.

Norman, the Dancing Master

Scottish country dancing –
a safe, non-sexual way
for boys and girls to interact,
to learn the social graces
of holding without grabbing,
of seeing a favourite in the arms
of someone else, without jealousy,
knowing she'd come round again.
And the skills of co-ordinating movement
to music, following intricate patterns
and sequences of steps, when to twirl,
when to set to your partner.

Mr MacCaig was the best teacher for it,
loved ceilidhs – I know that now
having spoken to the sons and daughters
of his summer friends in Assynt.
Tall, arrow-thin, with a strong, rather harsh voice,
he and Miss Brown would spin the shellacs
on the wind-up gramophone.

With me it didn't take. I fumbled and stumbled,
staggered in dizzy shy circles with girls
who'd mastered rhythm, could count up to eight,
and then another eight, and another,
and all without moving their lips.
I hated these sessions, still can't dance
formal steps. I prefer improv, jazz,
and wish he'd taught me free verse.

A corner of a foreign field

I land at Luton, full Highland-dressed.
Security waves me to by-pass the barrier,
knowing my shiny buckle, silver buttons,
would set off all the alarms.
He doesn't frisk my kilt, and I've left
the sgian dubh at home.

I'm picked up and driven to the venue
for my speech – a library launch.
With time to spare I wander round
the campus. My eye is caught
by a cohort of men kilted like me,
and ladies in cream taffeta –
Scottish country dancers.

"Which part of Scotland
are you from?" I ask one
"Milton Keynes," he says,
as if there's anywhere else.

Growth
in memory of Edwin Morgan

Drop a seed into the ground,
add a little water,
and growth seems inevitable,
barring accidents and incidents.

And the seeds form shoots
and roots from little clumps
of rapidly dividing cells.
Seven generations of cell lines,

seven sets of divisions,
and you have an adult plant –
lettuce, turnip, courgette
or baby tree.

And within these green machines
the germs of the next generation,
like matryoshka dolls, ripe
for fertilisation.

It's the same in the animal kingdom,
seven generations to produce
a final image, the complete being.
Not finished, for that would be an end.

We still grow, but at a slower rate,
adding bulk, experience, wisdom,
making our own seeds; a production line
of people, like us, but different.

The seeds of the mind grow too,
and a poet's words with luck live on,
an expanding shell of shared awareness,
from Mercury to Saturn and beyond.

Manoeuvres

A lippy Tornado blinks over the house
across the road. It's over mine and gone
before the sound hits. A rasping roar
I hear terrified the poor of Belgrade,
the leaky armies of Iraq – twice –
and the hot population of Herat.

It has the power to scare me – two big engines
and reheat – but it doesn't, the way nobody bothered
about the drone of Dorniers bumbling off
to bomb Coventry, if you were on that side
of the conflict.

A laser aligns on nothing,
a featureless co-ordinate on the surface of the sea,
a point with meaning only to a distant Controller
and a targeting computer. Maybe a porpoise
is charmed by this brief damned spot;
maybe a livid squid tries and fails
to mimic neodymium's ruby glow. More likely
even plankton are indifferent.

Somewhere, between Brunt Hill and the May Island,
a mission is accomplished, switches click, plane tips,
turns on a wing, streaks back over the Debateable Lands,
follows valley twists and speed-bump hills, to smear rubber
on some Southern tarmac.

Nobody dies here, no-one is threatened, locals don't look up.
Even sheep nibble on, and nervous horses show more fear
of a smoky two-stroke. We're all in training, knowing
stoic apathy's what we're good at; a survival trait essential
when the enemy's undefined, and can't be bombed away.

St Abb's Head

The ocean loafs, pale-blue,
flat, under a flat blue sky
white-lined by high jets.

Paired fulmars duvet each other,
warming a grassy hollow
to receive their precious futures.

On bare, shit-stained ledges
the guillemots gather,
black coats cinched against the cold.

Herring gulls soar over frosted crags
and pipits dash for hatching flies
on the rabbit-cropped meadow.

The day walks from Starney Bay
to the old salmon station
at Pettico Wick.

Eiders share their dives
with black-suited men,
shrink-wrapped in rubber, bubbling.

From our cliff-top vantage
we picture their dimming descent,
their time-tabled weightlessness.

Baldred on the Bass

The cold in this cell rises
from my damp feet to my tonsure,
from my naked arse hanging over
the stone lintel to my tongue
numbed from prayers and curses.

The blessing is, the only blessing is,
that the smell is lighter in winter,
less pungent. The seabirds keep me
company at times.
Last Spring a solan's beak
poked through the bars, those unlidded eyes
staring, as if I might be a herring
he'd missed.

I could compose a canticle
to these javelined white travellers.

I am sick of sour flat bread
baked on stones, smoked
by burning seaweed, and my drink,
not the sweet small beer of Auldhame
but rainwater puddled in rocks,
channelled to my bucket.

Some days Summer feels as far away
as Hell.

Backyard dreams

Allotments occupy
the tatty ends of towns,
derelict banlieues where
the rail lines run.

Behind the rusted sidings,
decrepit rolling stock, lie
      stockpiles of coal and salt,
      builders' merchants, scrap cars –
      each once an owner's dream –
      industrial estates strangers
      to prosperity, distribution depots,
      failed factories,
      smokeless brick chimneys,
      half-hearted signs for strippers
      and lap dancers whose nights
are long past bedtime.

Green patches in the middle of all this
proclaim each hut's a home from home.
Garden furniture adorns a living room
where vegetables flourish at the core
of dreams, seeds of hope sown
in these districts of disappointment.

Corruption

The water butt stank. Sure manure
betimes smells bad – know how
fetid retted comfrey gets?

This was worse. Think pigshit,
double it and add ammonia.
Ever been to a tannery?

Ever stood downwind
of a renderer? Abattoirs
are pine-fresh when compared,

but odour words are watery
components of our language.
Too often similes have to do.

This was, then, a Gothic concoction,
a multi-layered reek, symphonic
in complexity; feculence

and putrefaction the major themes,
and no relieving leitmotif –
really not nice.

The thought of sourcing
this noisesomeness
had us gagging,

but someone had to clean
the allotment's Augean stable.
Gingerly forking, I snagged

a weight and undrowned it.
A cat, black now but forever
unlucky, squelched out

on the straw by the shed
like a birth gone wrong.
Another swirl, just to make sure,

hooked a second stinker
further down the line
to dissolution.

It took a long time
to trust the vegetables
watered from this whiffy barrel.

Growing fruitful

On the third day the blossoms start to shrink.
Purpose served, they furl their flags. Beauty begins

to shrivel, wrinkle back to the flower's core
where bees have been, have dusted pollen from comb feet

onto the sticky pads, each one a gateway
to an apple of tomorrow. Two weeks ago

a frost snarled round my garden, turned pink to brown
before the warmth of dawn could heal, declaring

this will be a No-Peach Year. Soon enough I'll sit
under an arc of cherries with a cup of fragrant wine

distilled from my old plum tree.
He's a fine specimen now, settled in maturity,

reliable, a steady cropper. I'll drink to him
as I write new poems.

After the break

The difference between "HELP!" and _{"Oh, help me"}
is a profound thing, and it's midnight. A woman
in a unit across the corridor, disturbed, confused,
and I'm in no condition to diagnose, much less to help.

Besides, the nurses' station is closer to her than I am,
and if they think she needn't be helped, that's it. A doctor
comes in to my dark unit, switches on a dim light,
checks I'm awake and takes my whispered history.

She measures my temperature, blood pressure,
asks if I've eaten – I haven't – takes a note
of allergies. It's a routine that should have happened
before the shift change, but what can you do?

The nurse has rigged up a sling on a pole
from bandages and tape. It'll help reduce swelling
before the op, keeps my arm up. The proper support
has a Name, but they've run out, and this will do.

I'm used to turning in the night, but now I can't
and it's hard to sleep. I doze, time to time.
3am and a new nurse checks me. The sling
needs tightening, so he does it. Another doze.

5am, another shift change, and some kind
of morning routine is kicking in, on all the units
of the ward. Another check, another history.
I forget when the woman stopped calling,

but it's quiet now. Tea is offered to the two other men
in the 4-bed unit, but not to me – I'm NBM. I'm told
I'm on the first list, should be done by 10. It's OK,
I'm in no position to question. I'm not thirsty anyway.

34

Anaesthetist pops in, takes my history, tells me
what will happen. Surgeon does his early rounds,
tells me what he'll do to me, assistant takes my history.
Some time in the morning I sleep, drowsy with painkillers.

Morning slips by, lunch is not offered. Doctor checks me,
says it'll be the afternoon list. I can't go anywhere.
Then the porters come in, wheel my bed into the lift,
take me down to the prep room. Do they still use pentothal?

I wake in a new ward, having forgotten the names
of all the staff who've introduced themselves to me
in the last 24 hours. I'm offered tea, but it comes up
immediately. I can't stop vomiting. I lose a lot

of the fluids I haven't been drinking, and they decide
I'll have to live with them for another night.
I react badly to a pain-killer, BP drops
and I feel faint. I forget its Name.

I need to pee but, cast on one arm,
drip and support on the other,
I can't fasten my gown behind me.
Past caring that my arse is showing,

I shuffle across the ward. On the way back
a nurse ties the tapes 'to give me some dignity'
but that's not what I need most.
I want to go home, and the next day,

after a ward round that doesn't happen,
and a couple of phone calls
to get round Irregularity of Procedure,
I do.

Meditating in North Uist

Birdsong woke me: the dawn chorus
seeped from room to room through the paper walls

of the old poet's house. I drank tea and began
these notes on our journey.

We were four – Alec, Rebecca, Barney the dog
and myself, long in years, rich in memories.

I did not want to make of this a ceremony
but there were elements – we adapted local custom,

brought our crafts and knowledge to the tasks,
learned as much as taught.

We travelled North and West, through the glens
and sunlit mountains to the coast, then made the voyage

through the narrows between Mull and mainland,
across a blue Minch to the lands the Norse called

the Southern Isles. Crossing causeways we met our guide
and after a hundred Passing Places reached our cottage,

on an island, off an island, off an island, off the home islands,
the westmost point where our folk still live. Nothing beyond us

but white waves, green seas. Here we rested.

Then to Langais new wood, to meet our pupils,
our young poets. We found the seven trees –

pines, rowan, juniper, and in the gash blasted
by the Great Storm of twenty-ought-five, a holly,

defiant among death and destruction. Seven birds
sang in the tops, and on the ground we chose

seven plants. Their names, linked to points
on a magic map, to be woven in a cloth of poems.

At the top of the wood lies a giant dolmen,
its massive slab slumped beside its prone supports.

This is one vertex of the Langais triangle,
three stone mysteries left by the old ones.

A standing stone marks the mooring for sea-borne pilgrims.
Across the hilltop is the chambered cairn, a mound of pale stones.

We bow our heads below the lintel-stone
and enter the emptied tomb on hands and knees,

a form of reverence forced by circumstance,
but I go no further than the entrance.

I am overcome with the certainty, deeply felt,
that under the hill is no place for the living,

and I am not yet ready.

My Eiheiji temple is the Hut of Shadows by Lochmaddy,
a new thing, a stone chamber in the sound of the wind.

Here we sit, in total darkness, a form of zazen Dōgen
would have recognised. Slowly, as our eyes adjust,

a picture from the world of light outside emerges,
projected on the opposite wall.

We draw our own conclusions.

Notes:
This poem was written after visiting North Uist with Alec Finlay as part of The Road North project. Part of the project involved matching Scottish places with the places mentioned by Bashō in his great work Oku no hosomichi. Bharpa Langais was identified with Eiheiji.

Dōgen was the founder of the Soto Zen sect, which practises zazen – sitting meditation. He established the order at Eiheiji.

The Hut of Shadows is an artwork, featuring a camera obscura, built by Chris Drury on the shore at Lochmaddy.

Uisticity

By the side of the door, on the concrete stoop,
a circle of equal-sized mussel shells,
a blue whorl, noses pointing in
to the centre where a white stone rests.

You stretch out an arm, curl it in
enfolding the grey bay, the little
island, rock-ringed eider haven
beyond fox-reach. It's yours.

The beach an unlikely white,
a carbonate snow, drifting
in the wind's whisper, off
a green sea. Paddling is good

for feet too long enclosed
in unforgiving leather. The land
is defined by flowers and grass.
It too is beach, with a skin of life.

Smudges far out fail to resolve
into the islands we know are there,
remain as unvisited names, but
the birds take our wishes over.

Implements of wood, stone, bone,
a culture of cast-ups fashioned
to trim a harsh life, fish-hooks,
cut-out combs, necessary beads,

in glass-fronted cases in a house
of history, walled with art and memory,
fragments of found lives, splinters
of belonging, ways of wondering.

Flat-pack days self-assemble
without diagram or Allen key,
in an order that feels right.
Somehow, the parts fit. Trig.

Flax

Wee blue flowers filled the fields until wilting time, then cut off low,
seeds shaken into waiting baskets and the long stems water-rotted
so the fibres fell free of the slime.

And the fibres dried, washed, dried again, teased, split thin,
combed and singled, spun into threads, threads into yarn,
yarn woven into fine linen, a rough buff cloth, bleached white
and pummelled to soften, for shirts, sheets and table linen.

And the seeds ground till the oil oozed out, husks caked for the beasts
in barn and stable, a greasy satisfaction, and the smelly oil
boiled once for paint, twice for putty, thrice for linoleum,
air-blown, mixed with pine rosin, cork dust, wood flour,
poured on a backing of woven jute that began its journey in fields
by the Hoogli River. Floorcloth for battleships, stained and printed
for homes, a durable cover and a bugger to lay well.

You always got a man in to lay it, with fearsome knives
and a hot iron to joint the tougher rebates and recesses
of your kitchen. Afterwards, the whole house smelled of it
for weeks, and relatives, neighbours, sniffed and said
how much they liked the smell, reminded them
of their childhoods, an industrial freshness, new.

Bog cotton

Wrappit in ma downie canach sark
Ah feel nae win, nor fear nae cauld.

A kin o girss, ye say?
Ae silky tassle, snaw-bricht,
bends wi the warslin westers
an chitterin northlies
bit stauns abin the muir.
Nae heich, nae sae heich
as hae them pu'ed oot.

Some fite flags is no
fur giein up, bit gauin oan.

The desired effect

The girl's breasts were not so much cupped
by her bra, as platformed by it.
She watched you watching them tremble
with each of her small movements,
and she moved a lot, even standing still.

Her mother talked later
about the hormone levels
of teenage girls, a waft of desire
you could almost smell.
Cath was, you thought,
nostalgic for the time
her own attractive power
was as strong as this;
when her need could rouse
a want in watchers.

Then you looked at yourself,
trying to equate the sensations
of surfboard and surf,
knowing now the trough of passion
and yearning for a lost crest.

Inspiration

Between forgetting to breathe in
and remembering to breathe out,
I see you. It's the first time,
the only time, since the last time,
and the blood thumps in my ears,
pulses in my neck. Surely others
can see it swelling?

I am sick, faint, perpetually unsettled,
a balloon below my ribs.
All is pressure, mounting.
I am madness, tempted
to cast off restraint,
dismiss rules and precedent,
the dreary concerns
of passionless days,
careless of consequence.

You never were my dream;
fantasy is unearned income.
You are real, body. I am tight air,
circled, confined, close to you,
but not as close as desire
would take me.

In the studio of introspection
I have rehearsed speech,
conversations like chess moves
where I am always knight.
Then I see you, and I am silence,
an inner stammer, dumbed by your eyes.

44

Highlights from the scented lamps
flicker as you hold my gaze.
I look to the flames
reflected in the red gems
round your slim neck,
like pomegranate seeds
captured by gold threads,
clenched as is my ruby heart.

It's you, it is only you.
Let me stroke your firelit jewels,
close your firestruck eyes;
let me begin to breathe.

Roughneck

I am Cancer
so I do not like cats. Just so
you don't misunderstand,
I'm not fond of dogs
(or dog products) either. I once
owned a gold fish. It wasn't
very bright.

At the time of my birth Venus
was in the ascendant, as
she usually is, which determines
my love of and for the sea.

I have never married,
but rely on transactions
to tend my wanton wishes.

Every day, without fail,
I imagine an oil rig.
It's a semi-sub, surfaced,
with its three big legs jacked
in the air, a tri-mast schooner
on tow in the Tay Firth, or maybe Beauly,
or spudded in, hunkered on a hardground
in the Viking Graben.

I am bald, from over-combing
in teen years. I flicked back
hair slick with scented emulsions
until there was nothing but air
to bring forward.

In Chinese terms, I'm a horse,
hard-working, quiet, a plodder
hauling the plough
through recalcitrant clay. The year
makes me a Water Horse –
Hippo aquaticus. No comments
from the back of the class.

I've always felt drawn
to Ganesha, initiator, breaker
of obstacles; not what you'd call
a natural dancer, Strictly speaking,
with that elephant head
on a human body, but he gets by.

Shaking the yarrow stalks
the last time, I read
that firmness and modesty
are prerequisites for harmonious joy.

Luck, on the other hand,
has nothing to do with it.
It's how you play
the card in hand
that counts in the end,
and mine's the five of clubs.

Allergic reaction

I scrabble in the bottom of my pocket,
among the small coins,
for the half-tablet of anti-histamine
I broke off earlier. I can't take
a whole one, it makes me drowsy,
no matter that the instructions
say it doesn't. I hate waking
with that drugged feeling,
throat dry, eyes slow to focus,
thoughts even slower.

I wash it down with a chug
of wheat beer – hefe Weizen –
note its silken translucency,
taste an agreeable sourness.
I've tried the Kristall kind,
enjoyed it, liked being able
to see the bubbles rise,
but the bottled brew
lacks the fresh bite
of draught – vom Fass –
like the stuff we drank
in Regensburg. That was the night
before the Czech border,
the lines of blonde whores
working the German truckers
on the Çesko side. God, they were beautiful,
really beautiful, really desperate
for dollars, D-Marks, a ride
to the 'Free' West.

On, past the wrought-iron gates
of the Pilsner Urquell brewery in Plzeň,
and the next day in Prague, across the Vltava,
lunching on tripe soup, pork with potato
dumplings, a half-litre of U Fleku's dark brown
sticky miracle – the best beer
I've tasted. Now we're getting
somewhere.

The concept of Beinn Dorain

From the road it's perfect,
a green cone, a Scottish Fuji, but that
's just its benign flank.
Close to, Beinn Dorain and
Beinn an Dothaidh, twin peaks,
are linked by a rock rampart,
a cliff where ravens croak and soar.

The path's a scramble
up a shaky river bed;
loose, wet gravel the perfect pediment
to turn an ankle, jar a knee.

Grassy banks are spiked
with the yellow stars of asphodel
and polka-dotted with heather.
Here and there – mostly there –
Norman's frogs shimmy through
the dew-dropped tussocks.
They are as he described them,
multi-coloured and numerous,
fattened on the midges who, sadly,
still out-number them.

Along with the flask of 'Iron Buddha' tea,
the salmon sandwiches and the bananas,
I'm carrying two dead poets and a legend
in my rucksack. Iain and Norman I knew,
Duncan ban MacIntyre only in translation.
They get me thinking (again) about age,
about my own age. Each hill hereabouts
has a flat shoulder near 3,000 feet,
where summit glaciers rested
before plunging down to carve the glens.
This is where the saxifrages start -

the white, starry ones, and on the rocks
the purple ones.
That's where I think I am now,
on one of life's high shoulders,
gawking at mountains,
starstruck by flowers.
A small flock of sheep grazes here,
each stolid ewe with a skittish lamb,
exploring, then running back to mother.
At the foot of the final ridge
I look up at an old hare nibbling,
long ears turned to catch my sounds.

At the summit, the hare and I see all
that the map has promised,
high peaks and deep glens.
One glen's obscured by a grey haze,
where someone's getting a drenching,
no doubt deserved. Before it's my turn,
because I probably deserve it too,
I stumble down to the enlarging village
at the Bridge of Orchy.

I haven't 'bagged' this Munro;
it remains unconquered,
like its unclimbed partner,
but I've shared its space,
seen its bulk part the winds,
and wring out their moisture.
High above the frog-line
there's no need to debate
the meaning of mountains.

The ascent of magic

On Suilven's summit ridge
I'm a four-year old, climbing
a spiral staircase too big for me.
The treads are fine but the risers
are a stretch too far and facing out
on a thousand-foot fall
too easily imagined.

Still, having traversed that
there's the domed grassy top
and a cairn, but the peak experience,
the real triumphs, were below:
the switchback bog slog, the scramble
up to the bealach, and suddenly -
a projection of wonder,
as the whole of northern Scotland
changed from map to photo
in an everlasting instant.

Islets; a haibun

We drive up the central hilly spine of the main island, called Mainland, heading for the Yell ferry. We arrive in Toft just after sailing time, but the crew have seen our car coming down the hill, and wait for us. The long isle of Yell is shrouded in thick mist, and we see only peat bog on either side of the road. At Gutcher we catch the boat for Unst with time to spare. This island appears greener, more fertile, cultivated. We skirt the hamlet of Baltasound and make for the Keen of Hamar, our northernmost destination.

The hillside appears barren, a field of angular stones, but this is a special place, worth the journey of a thousand miles. The snakeskin-scaled rocks here were once emplaced deep within oceanic crust – the Unst ophiolite. Our Hamar field consists of weathered serpentinite debris, and over the hill are abandoned talc and chromite mines, but what we've come to see are the flowers.

In this bleak, impoverished landscape grows a concentration of Arctic-Alpine rarities usually found on high mountains, and one found here and nowhere else. We tiptoe over the rubble, for fear of treading on one of these scattered botanical gems. At each new discovery we call across to each other to come and look. In this fashion we move, slowly, stooping, zigzagging, from Moss Campion to stunted Purple Orchid, from Norwegian Sandwort to Edmonston's Chickweed, to Mountain Everlasting - a hoard of beautiful survivors in a scree of desolation.

Home now, I walk on beach pebbles to reinforce memory.

     lea of a boulder
     slow clump of pink blossoms
     trembles in the wind

The Lost Valley

Walk down a steep slope to a stream
in a deep-cut gorge, crossed
by wooden footbridge. Look down,
see brown water gleam transparent
gliding over submerged stones,
plunging down short falls
spitting frothy bubbles.

The track turns sharp up on the other side,
twists between granite guardians.
Then comes a boulder-ballet
on the coggly crown of a giant rockfall.
The last obstacle's a narrow ledge,
with no net below.

Suddenly here's the hidden glen,
flat-floored with river gravel
too wide for this wee burn
to have laid it. A rowan grows
out of a house-sized boulder,
heather patterns and purples
the slopes, sparse grass tussocks
enough for wiry sheep.

All round, a ring of peaks
show their shadow sides
picked out by summer snowpatch.
Home is wherever you are
when you are most
yourself.

Ice Age

Down by the sea shore we saw no dark edge
to the white horizon. Pressure ridges
rose and fell with the tides,
creating temporary mountain ranges
with spiky summits. Far out, way beyond walking,
huge bergs growled and cracked on the swell,
pushed nearer by an unkind wind.
They streamed out from the Denmark Strait,
down the Sea of Labrador, across the track
of the dead Gulf Stream, these blue leviathans,
mountains of solid water.

Inland, we walked to the hills, foraging for firewood,
tramping through a fresh layer of powder snow,
avoiding the drifts and the cornices overhanging
the cliffs. Last year's snow poked through the crust
in places, wind-sculpted, sun-eroded, slowly compressing
as layer upon layer recrystallised to ice, and began to flow
down to the sea.

In the petrified forest, as the wind rose,
dead songbirds fell out of the trees.

Inner Time

Anchored tankers ride out
a dip in oil price, and the sine-wave tides.
The crew grease the slides
of the onboard Bofors gun,
prepare to repel pirates
swarming out from Crail lairs
or the balmy yards of Pittenweem.

A rented house in the dry Tortugas,
tending the fire and the maid's
remorseless nostalgia,
sodden with cooking sherry
and the yawning gulf of cocktail hour
between limitless sky
and the night's possibilities.

After tumultuous hours spent
with the domestic goddess,
breakfast was a slice of rustic bread,
crust flecked with grains and seeds,
topped with sour cherry preserve.

I once had a job restoring Crusader castles
to make fit for film sets. I sourced stone,
which, sawn in matched slices, veneered
the breeze blocks, fronted up
the rubble infill.

Bedraggled cat drags himself in
from a rainy night of fucking, yowling, scrapping,
bucket-sniffing, laps milk with backward-pointing
papillae, slumps for a fire-snooze, skin secreting
a vitamin precursor set by the sun.

Another day, another dolour.

Two At the Fishing

Home is a point on a dark, fuzzy line
way South, but you know where you are
– the screen tells you, minute by minute.

Shoalseeker sonar is switched off, not needed,
birds have shown you where the fish are,
moiling in a ball of panic.
Gannets Stuka down, stretch wings back
to strike the surface with spearpoint beaks.

There's a smell of fish in the air,
a sheen of light oil on the water.
Confetti of torn scales
catches the sun's scarce light
tumbling in winking seconds
into green depths, and darker.

Up surges the big one,
Fishfinder-General, fin whale,
turns on his side, shows off
his whitened right jaw,
pale as the throat pleats
which distend in a gulp
of water and herring,
a bird or two that misread
the force of his coming.

Tongue squeezes up,
presses water out
through a corset of bristly plates,
rolls back, pushes a wad
of fishmeat, fragments,
the odd beak and wing,
back to the open and shut case
of his gullet.

The splashback shakes your boat,
shakes you. You nod your head
in admiration, knowing this whale
is a finisher – two more sea-bites
and your shoal is gone.
You turn your helm away,
leave the nets unshot,
and rev off on a new heading.
Plenty more fish in the sea
this good summer drave.

The Book of Instructions

Remove the outer wrapping
from the box in which
your new lover was delivered.
Carefully detach the polystyrene
packing material – those lightweight scraps
of remaindered dreams and memories
of earlier loves new lovers
always bring with them -
poor dears, they can't help it.

Familiarise yourself with the safety features
of your acquisition, especially the circuit breaker
guarding the core from emotional overload.
You have to build the current up gradually
with this new model. Remember how
the last love failed, spectacularly?
You can't afford a repeat. Study how
Tab A fits Slot B smoothly and firmly.

This is a complex offering, so don't expect
everything optimal at the start. Don't trade in
the minute a feature fails. This sometimes happens
until all working parts are fully bedded in.
Repair, lubricate, nourish, accessorize, add
new components, grow with your lover.

This product does not carry a lifetime guarantee
but it has been designed to give you years of happiness,
and we hope you will be completely satisfied.

Leaving the nests

Ant tunnels fill with excitement
and pheromones. Fat
winged alates jostle past
sexless workers, fighters,
boil out of the entrance, take off
for their nuptial flight.

In the sky silent gulls
fly open-mouthed
through the swarms,
jinking, dipping, tumbling,
taking their formic harvest,
a pungent feast. Those missed
pair in the air, fall to ground,
shed once-used wings. Males die,
but fertilised queens crawl off
to found new empires.

Dragonfly's message under the Linden Tree

Before my father's time no Swedes used last names:
you were your father's son, your father's daughter.
He was a modernist, adopted the new fashion
and the name Linnaeus, after the tree in the rectory garden.

He taught me the names of plants,
scolded me when I forgot them,
so I took mnemonic routes to improve recall,
two words to bring back a phrase
from my mental nebula.

My Systema is based on sex, of course:
how many parts, how arranged,
how positioned? These questions
lead to natural groupings, like with like,
like with similar, and so families are formed.

Under the massive Linden Tree
sugary drops of sap fall from aphids' arses,
attracting ants, wasps, beetles, bugs,
and the bigger beasts that feed on them.
Hornets drone through the branches,
a dozen kinds of bird flutter and pounce,
and the green flashes of hawker dragonflies
zip through summer air, fearsome jaws
clasping hapless victims. I have read the message
of their bodies, and they are classified.

Lepus

Lowland racers course, flat-eared,
across sprouting wheat, jinking
past open-mouthed hounds,
whose backs arch like living leaf-springs.

A childhood memory: walking down Caerketton,
a brown shape leapt from heathery form,
dashed across contours, and it's my heart
today still hammers.

Rounding a bend in the path
that skirts Loch Turret, dog-end
of a long winter, a confident hare squats,
grey fur patched with snow,
vibrissae twitching, nosing my nature
and the narrowing distance to flight.

At the reverse bend, brother hare,
or maybe sister, and where track forks
another. I remember Frost, but forget
which direction made all the difference.
No matter. Either, today, will be perfect.

And Ben Chonzie's broad whaleback top,
tussocked and tasselled with sedge
and bog cotton, is dotted with shapes
that lollop or sit still, hare after hare
blowing in the lovely wind.

Coronation chickens
(After a photograph by Henri Cartier-Bresson)

Asleep on the headlines
a man sprawls, partied out.
From the plinth, way pre-Gormley,
legs dangle. A young Mr Pastry
raises eyes in the direction of yesterday.
Beside him Mary Poppins holds a bag
the size of Belgium on her lap,
praying for the shy new king –
God Save him.

A schoolboy in belted gabardine
and badged cap, stares moodily at Henri
taking the picture. It's the one
non-boring non-event of the day.

Two governesses stand poised for capture
if he moves a muscle,
but he won't. The cap sits as uneasily
on his head as the crown
upon another – it's the same
coronation. Across the square
lions guard the front
we'll soon call home.
Over the water, armies
whet bayonets, oil trumpets
for the fanfares of war,
but nobody's looking, not today.

Parting; a ghazal

The rock-swirled sea's a whisked-egg foam,
and at the tide's limit I leave you here.

I walk in celebration of the wind,
and at the road's end I leave you here.

Late season harvests from the hedgerows;
sweet, dark, are the berries I leave you here,

And if sweet juice should linger on your lips
let it stand for the kiss I leave you here.

If I could make the time run slower, I'd still
want more with you, before I leave you here.

The cold finds gaps between scarf and coat,
and so it's tightly wrapped I leave you here.

I know the moisture in your eyes is wind-born,
and not because you're sad I leave you here,

But as I turn away my head and head for home
I know I leave a better part of me, as I leave you here.

To Go

Striding along Market Street,
briefcase in one hand,
brown-bagged bagel
with a bitten crescent
and a balanced paper cup
in the other,
the business breakfastman
takes a suck of coffee
through the sipper lid.

His steps don't falter,
dodging the bum
with the market trolley
returning empties for nickels.
He has purpose
and a certain style
that states, by shoeshine,
suitcrease, shades, neat
tie, that though he's merely walking,
he has surely arrived.

The last of the little green men

From words of Shakespeare much knowledge
can be gained. Difficult to see the future is,
but these plays often insights contain.
The rise of the Dark Side consider: Lear
and Hamlet fine parallels provide.
Encroaching blindness, dying, a poisonous madness,
betimes recall the wit of Solo and Lord Vader's rage.
Descent and resurrection, all Campbell's themes,
loss of the mother, jealousy of the father,
discovery of the unknown Other,
all archetypal are.

I too an archetype am.
How many the Mekon remember?
My green nest-mate, long retired,
over his cloned Treen army hovered
on an inverted iron, war on Venus directing.
Defeat by Dan Dare, Skywalker's ancestor,
inevitable was. Good over evil
triumphs always. My words mark.

Back to my egg return I shall,
to the nest wherein was I laid.
Whence we came, thereto shall we all
back go. Time backwards runs.
Lost labour's love, Caesar Julius,
all Dreams of night's midsummer,
upon the stage their hour fret
and strut. A walking shadow
life is. More no.

Solar power
After Allen Ginsberg's Sunflower Sutra

We've walked together, you and I, along the summer streets
of many cities: smoggy Beijing, bright Rome, uneasy Los
Angeles – so many places, so many pavements, our hot feet
taking us along the world's dusty streets.

On a back street in Barcelona, with the dark stains of dried
piss on the pavement, and walking with downcast eyes to
not tread where dogs have defecated out of range of poly
bags, a corner plot was cultivated, and here a sunflower
blazed in the canyon between high apartment blocks.

We walked on, past the pavement table outside the grubby
bar. Who would sit here, in the dust, the grime, and the traffic
smells? Two do, smoking, where it's still allowed, two glasses
of red wine at the focus, where no-one's looking.

Near the seafront the road widened, edged with municipal
beds of colour, a regiment of blues, whites and reds, a flat
carpet where we want height, and yellow. It's hot, we look
for shade, crave a parasol, a hat, rain.

Remember the oilfields of France? Hectares of gold, enough
for an army of painters, enough to blind the sun, a solar
system on each plant.

Remember cycling these roads, corn one side, sunflowers the
other? And the field of hemp, grown for its fibre, licensed, the
low THC variety, but high anyway?

Look at the names of yellows: cadmium, lemon, primrose,
sulphur, chrome. None of them says sunflower. Van Gogh
used cadmium, a known carcinogen, but not then, a yellow to
die for.

Going back to my beginning, a city centre tenement, chill in winter, sticky in summer, out front a small patch of soil, a few metres of grey dust, and tied to a cane, a spindly scaffold of stem, big leaves, and a head that faces East.

City-kid, sun-worshipper, sunburned seaside blisterer and the smell of pink calamine lotion, universal soother, nights without turning, sleeping, days in long clothes and not regretted, not for a minute, UV-A and B penetrating, warming, a fusion factory 93 million miles away and never close enough to these northern lands where winter lingers too long and summer days, though long, are never long enough.

> Shine, from the tops of your green columns.
> Shine, from the sky's blue eye.
> Apollo, rise, strike up your lyre.
> Amaterasu, come out of the sulking cave.
> Sol, slip slowly across the sky,
> Helios, glow in the burnished mirror.
> Svarog, enlighten the North.
> Belenos, be fire in the sacred circle.
> Surya, illuminate the golden scriptures.
> Ra, bring us safely across the heavens to the infinite
> depths of the starry night.
> And rise again.

Tondo

It was some years back
but I remember it well.
The Gallery called and asked me
to confirm some plants

in a Raphael. I'd been working
on the old Herbals, knew
my plants. Piece of cake,
I thought, and so it was.

The painter was no Füllmauer,
no Gesner, but his skills
were up to the job.
For the most part,

standard European flora;
meadow flowers mostly,
and strewn at foot,
understated but accurate,

unmistakeable strawberries,
trefoil leaves, toothed,
white flowers and red hearts
among the foliage.

Fragaria vesca, I'd know it
anywhere, a wildwood berry,
as tasty then as now. The answers
were easy; the questions

have me stumped, still. Why
strawberries? What have they to do
with the Christian story? In which
Gospel do they figure?

Do they echo Christ's sweet
bleeding heart? Or the blood
to come? I didn't know then,
still don't. The iconography

can't be separated from the art,
and that's bound tightly to a faith
I don't share. The story is told
in many ways – an infinite variety –

the parents, the child, but a child
with a destiny overhanging,
a fate, and the sharp sweet tang
of strawberries. These ones,

note this well, not the modern,
swollen, watery confections,
but closer to the Alpine kind,
tart and acid, and thinly scattered.

The palm tree's out of place; Middle East
in Europe, not native, not even close,
as this one's a date palm,
Phoenix dactylifera, needing

more heat than Italy provides
to make its bone-hearted fruit,
the one-dimensional taste
of soft, sugary pap.

What the artist knew,
had experienced, were the sweets
of the forest floor, scarce,
in the semi-shade,

hard to find, harder to forget,
like the ones in Raphael's image,
carmine drops in a landscape
limned by belief.

Talking of Michelangelo

I'm thinking about Michelangelo
while observing a Calder mobile
in the garden of the Reina Sofia.

A spiderling floats by
all eight legs tightly clenched
on its personal air line.

This is the season for them -
remember how many
bannered out from the power lines
at St Abb's Head?

But I digress: M. would not
have calculated moments,
points of balance
about a central point.

The main focus, for him,
was a body's centre of gravity,
the line the weight takes
from hair on head
to pillar limbs,
and each arch of the foot
a bow pulled for stand or leap.

A flung arm shifts, opposing
a trunk muscle;
an effort of will springs
and unconscious tensions
stabilise the body's poise.

Would he have dismissed this thing
of foils and nerveless steel?
A child's toy, maybe,
the easy virtues of a metal fulcrum
and welded bars. What's harder
is to uncover from Carrara block
the body parts and attitudes
that mimic, in waxy stone,
the flesh and intent
of human form,
stilled.

Confession

I'm like, "Shut up, shut the fuck up.
There's naebdy here. Honest."
An she's like, "He's in there,
Ah ken the basturt's there."
An I'm like, "He's no,
he's went hame oors ago."
An she's like, "Well he's no there
noo. WHERR IS E?"
So ah goes, "How the fuck
wid ah ken?"
An she's like, "Well it wis your throat
e hud is tongue haufwey doon
last time ah seen um. Hoor."

Well, ah um afraid that wis when
ah lost it com-fuckin-pletely.
Ah opent the door and wellied hur
wi the first hing that came tae haund.

An that is why, Miss,
she's got taen tae Hospital
wi a facefu o prickles
frae wir shoe-scraper,
ken, 's like a hedgehog.
It wisnae ma fault.
It wis jist there,
ken likesay thon guy
that climbed Everest says –
because it's fuckin there.
An hoo wis ah tae ken
the base wis cast iron? At least
it gave her man time
tae scoot oot the back door.
Preemature evacuation,
ah cries it.

Working Mothers

Monday morning, kids crêched,
time to hit the gym
for a weekly workout.

Time to catch
the latest chat,
as you run for dear life

facing the mirror
of yesterday's extra helping,
seeing tomorrow's toned

and youthful body;
squeezing out the weekend's toxins,
working up a sweat,

a schedule to tuck and tighten,
to firm and reform your figure,
recover your before-baby body.

Row, run, step, push,
the cycle of exercise freewheels
to the sounds of rap and chatter.

Meanwhile, in the corner,
a puffing Gran tries to reset
her own odometer

to ten years back,
hoping for twenty more,
betrayed by connective tissue

which snaps when it used
to stretch, by ballooning veins
and the hourglass streaming faster.

In the plant cemetery

This is where people bring their disasters –
the pot plant drowned by over-watering,
the tender shrub left outside a day too long
so the frost bit the cells in the soft stem,
turning it into smelly mush,
the seedlings in the glasshouse
that didn't survive your holiday
fortnight in the Bahamas.

They can be thrown out, of course,
dumped in recycling bin or composter,
but that's an undignified end,
without ceremony or memorial.

Better to bring them here,
stand before the corpses
on an unadorned aluminium shelf –
no flowers please, for that would be tasteless –
then after a suitable pause
for remembrance and reflection,
close the curtain on failure.

At night, the air shimmers with the glow
of ghostly bouquets, haunting fragrances.

Walking in Glencanisp

Snowblind from the apple blossom's garden glare
I turn, as I have so often, to wilder walks.

This strata's as ancient as the world itself,
and the carpet's starred with tormentil and violet.

Past the belt of planted Sitka spruce
the sky is mixed and busy, sun and shade.

Given choices, I'll sometimes be a follower, on paths,
and sometimes take a lead through trackless ground.

The route ascends heathery heughs and drops down dips
where tiny streams drain gurgling slopes.

In the palm of the landscape's hand, waters flow together
to top up a fortunate lochan, reflecting blue.

Birds sing, whether or not a person hears,
and the scents that I enjoy were made for others.

Placing foot before foot, the rhythm of walking
looses the mind to play, imagine, freewheel.

This is no journey with a definite end,
but a simple way of being in the now.

The Blues

When oxygen is cooled
to minus something or other
it becomes a pale blue liquid.

Pure water, frozen, is blue too.
Not blue as the sea in summer
is blue – that's just the sky

looking at itself in a mirror.
No, ice is blue, and the hue
intensifies with thickness.

Peer into a crevasse
on an alpine glacier:
the colour of danger,

of depth, is truest blue.
Up above, on a clear day,
the deepest shade is overhead,

at the horizon it pales
to the colour of a duck's
eggshell. The higher you go

the deeper it gets, and I recall,
in Lhasa, how the Potala's white bulk
was framed in a shade close to indigo.

Woad, a plant juice boiled
and sun-rinsed, became a potent dye
on Pictish skin and cloth.

And once, in a graveyard on the Somme,
two jet contrails crossed to make
a perfect Saltire. Alba, blue Alba.

Pictish brooch

On his cloak a lock
below the right shoulder
to hold the folds in place.

A salmon, Tay-caught,
tail at the hinge end,
mouth the hasp.

Stylised, incised in yellow metal,
the graven lines grasp
essence of wild rivers,

that leap up the fall,
time and again, over and over
and through to the spawning ground.

In the shallows, pushing
like an arrow, darting
in the gravel beds, covering eggs.

And then the fisherman
wades out, looks up for luck,
slides fingers forward,

lifts by the gills,
a full basket of pink flesh
to fuel his fellows.

Big man, this catcher,
throws the circle blanket
round his neck, pins it with a fish.

Complex numbers

I'm dipping again
into the fat maths book.
This is a world far stranger
than the one I think I know.

Physics deals with reals, rationals,
as weak forces and hazy particles
shift in and out of focus. Squiggle-atures
in cloud chambers can be seen, measured.

Below that, the laws of the universe
are written in an alphabet that needs
all the Latin letters, plus the Greek,
some Hebrew, and a notation that's not,
frankly, intuitive.

These half-understood
formulae and diagrams look convincing,
but I'm still not sure. We match concepts
to what we see around us,
and who can see infinity?

Everything's indefinite, indeterminate.
An uncertainty of position
or momentum denies the probability
of some things making sense
in eleven dimensions.

Gravity's felt as attraction, weight, a pull,
but it's really just the way
space-time curves
from you to me
in the time it takes
for tiny strings to spin
at right angles to everything.

What can we make
with quantum entanglement?
Beam me up, Scotty, I've got information
from a leaky black hole.

Where are we, in Hilbert space?
What's my eigenvalue?
Matter's only pale threads in a continuum
between the biggest bang
and our current points
of singularity.

My event horizon's
not absolute; it's pecked out
in white crests on a steel sea.
The book's shelved for later,
for some notional value of later.

CSI

A carrot in a courtyard
is all that's left to see.

Maybe, a fingertip search
of the paving blocks would turn up

two small lumps of eye coal,
a row of grit buttons,

and tied to the railing
a discarded scarf, flailing

in the stiff warm breeze
that killed the snowman.

Transactions

It was one of those
smoked salmon/scrambled egg breakfast
days, when anticipation/greed wins out
over common sense.

Dabbed my lips with impeccable linen.
A Dublin Day. Kicked the arse
of Old Year last night,
and always too ready to believe in rebirth.

Nothing crude mind – no turning into pumpkinned mice –
just a hope to uncover some finer facet
in a countenance too known
to be rendered capable of surprise.

Stepping out, then, into an optimistic morning
of Atlantic rain, past your man
leaning on his bronze cane, and cornering
brings me to an improbable recliner,

Anna Livia in a shower, God, Giant Anna
is the laid back shower, Liffey-water-feature.
A charming smile, I'll grant you,
purely charming. I pick

a small fillet from my teeth,
catch the Botanic Garden bus
to the soaked leafy suburbs
at Glasnevin, admire the big iron glasshouse,

stroll among the labels
where the green world is interpreted,
where summer weddings froth with snow
on the lawn, and corporates entertain.

It's a fair way to come
to seek the start of something new,
but then again it's not. Language difference
is confined to street signs

and the names of plants, universal binomials
in a tongue not spoken anywhere, and the coin
to pay for things pan-European, or almost so,
common currencies, no change given or expected.

Sitzpinkler

It's the German word
for men who sit to pee.
That'll be me then. It started
when I discovered the toilet lid
in our new home didn't stay up

That was ten years ago,
Now I squat without thinking,
find it awkward to stand
for a piss in public urinals,
hate the spray it makes,
that damp stain on pale trousers
advertising where I've been.

To the Moon-Viewing Height

The Philosopher's Walk's the temple axis
of Kyoto. Strung out along the channelled stream
each one, Shinto or Buddhist, has its own garden,
its own adherents.

The November air is warm and clear,
and we're surrounded by smiles
and shy politeness. We buy green-tea ice cream.

Hōnen-in has an austere beauty.
Through the thatched gate
gravel beds are raked in patterns.
In a water trough a single red flower floats.

Eikan-dō holds many halls, and here
we slip off shoes and shuffle along
the polished wood floors, view an exhibition
of paintings, ceramics, fabrics. Up the hill
a small shrine houses an androgynous Amida,
head turned as if to flirt with pilgrims.

Lunch is bought and eaten at Otoya-jinja,
a Shinto shrine, from a stall that sells
delicious o-bento, rich flavours
of cooked, raw and pickled vegetables, rice.
Here we watch worshippers who approach the doors,
bow, clap hands twice, pull the bell-rope, clap again,
bow and leave. As ceremonies go
it's simple, straightforward, self-conducted.

At the Silver Temple we enter the dry garden,
the Sea of Silver Sand, and a truncated cone,
the Kogetsudai, a conceptual platform
no-one steps on, to observe the moon,
pure Zen. The garden is fringed
by manicured Black Pine trees, stretching out
dark arms and green fingers. A winding path
leads past trickling water splashing
on autumn-coloured leaves, and ponds
reflecting Kyoto sky, Kyoto thoughts.

Vincent would have loved it.

The Three Day Moon had traversed
its low arc, risen and set inside an hour,
and the sky was never so dark
as that night at Glencanisp.

The familiar constellations –
Orion, Ursa Major, Cassiopeia –
had lost definition against a background
of as many points of light
as grains of white sand
on the beach at Achmelvich.
The Milky Way was a dim band
washed across the heavens,
and a bright planet
shone through a hazy spot
of unseen cloud.

We saw no shooting stars;
the only moving thing
the Space Station,
rushing along its 90-minute track,
a sine wave wedding the Earth.

We watched and watched
until we could take no more awe,
then went to bed to wait
for Suilven's sunrise spectacle.

Field notes, January to April

A cormorant follows the river's turns.
Even before the Lednock Burn joins it
the Earn is full, and flowing fast. I look
from the bridge, not even trying to estimate
the volume of water. It's been raining hard,
but there's also snowmelt.

The winter's snow came and went,
came and stayed, went, and came again.
Cold drifted on the winds below weeks
of grey skies. Thoughts of death,
knowledge of dying, tiptoed
from room to room, until morning,
a time told by the clock, not daylight.

****

Roe deer graze on the sloping hay field
in full view of unstoppable traffic.
Sometimes they are in the neat green rows
of winter wheat or spring barley.
I always count them, disappointed
if there are fewer than a dozen.

On a sunny bank a lemon froth of cowslips,
in the woods starry anemones, celandines
and shy violets. I remember a burn
in Twenty Shilling Wood, a spring walk,
a red deer seasonal casualty, slabs
of white flesh, tufts of sodden fur,
and antlers scavenged for a souvenir.

****

Changes started on a day with a lamb's coat sky.
I walked the riverbank in the scent of ramsons,
catkins on the birches. Water poured past
in near silence, gravity pulling it
to the Tay, and the sea's endless reservoir.

The hills were lit with noon sun.
Larch in the spruce, brown since fall,
took on a golden green tinge.
Bud-break was imminent in all the trees
along the bank, and the fresh ploughed earth waited.
In the house, she rose, dressed, ate a little.
Her body had decided it could, for now,
keep going.

Reading Tour

I check in at the digs, Friday afternoon,
see what the loo's like, where the shower,
walk round the town, suss the hall
for tonight's reading, think about phoning home, don't.

A meal with the host, small talk about small things,
agree again to be the warmer for the night's Featured Poet,
wonder why Italian's always the chosen cuisine,
why I'm nervous, why I continue to smile,
what I'll do if they don't like me?

It goes well for us both, then we answer questions,
the public ones, and later from advice-seekers.
We adjourn to the pub; the Featured Poet is a friend.
We share a laugh, a couple of halfs, we leave,
she to a distant cousin, me to my room, where, I now notice
the plywood wall has a wide gap between me
and the adjoining boarder, with his all-night radio show.

In the morning I try my four words of Czech
on the waitress from Prague who – and this is strange –
doesn't seem to understand. I fire a filthy look
at the sausages of my neighbour, check out,
drive to the next venue, dying for a sleep.

Grave Stone

Words weather. Lichen patches
blur the stone-cutter's art,
and no poet's work survives
the softening of time.